19

WICKED
WEATHER

ANITA GANERI

Scholastic Children's Books,
Euston House, 24 Eversholt Street,
London, NW1 1DB, UK

A division of Scholastic Ltd
London ~ New York ~ Toronto ~ Sydney ~ Auckland
Mexico City ~ New Delhi ~ Hong Kong

Editorial Director: Lisa Edwards
Senior Editor: Jill Sawyer
Art Director: Richard Smith

First published in the UK by Scholastic Ltd, 2008

Text copyright © Anita Ganeri, 2008
Illustrations © Mike Phillips 2008
Colour by Tom Connell
All rights reserved

ISBN 978 1407103 68 6

Printed and bound by Tien Wah Press Pte. Ltd, Malaysia

2 4 6 8 10 9 7 5 3 1

The right of Anita Ganeri and Mike Phillips to be identified as the author and illustrator of this
work respectively has been asserted by them in accordance with the Copyright, Designs and
Patents Act, 1988.

Contents

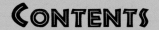

INTRODUCTION

Are you the sort of person who's always moaning about the weather? Well, you're not alone. People are always complaining it's too cold in winter, then too hot in summer. They rush for cover when they feel the tiniest drop of rain and get ruffled by the slightest breeze. What a bunch of drips! But forget battling to open your brolly or slapping on the suncream. It's time to brace yourself for some seriously stormy weather ahead. If the weather turned wild and woolly, how on Earth would you cope? DON'T PANIC! This horribly useful handbook contains everything you'll need to survive without throwing caution to the wind.

So, read on to find out…
• why you shouldn't go swimming in a thunderstorm
• what to do when a tornado starts to twist
• how to storm-proof your house for a hurricane
• how to stay cool as a cucumber in a heatwave
• what getting lost in a blizzard's really like.

SOME BLIZZARD, HUH?

And that's not all. This handy book's packed with terribly tasteless true stories about people who bravely weathered the storm. Not to mention those who looked the storm straight in the eye or found themselves in very deep water indeed.

But be warned. Despite having loads of new-fangled technology to play with, meteorologists (that's the posh name for weather scientists) can't always tell what the wicked weather's likely to do next. Storms sometimes blow in without warning and even the experts' forecasts aren't always foolproof. So you'll need to keep your wits about you and your eyes peeled for gathering storm clouds. Because we're not talking nice sunny days and blue skies here. Oh no. We're talking weather that'll rip your roof off or fry you to a crisp. This is weather that'll blow you away. Still keen to give wicked weather a whirl? Oh well, it's time to hang on to your hat...

WICKED WEATHER

It's a wild and windswept world out there, and it's about to get worse. Some people seem to enjoy getting soaked to the skin and find gale-force winds oddly bracing. But if your idea of good weather is clear blue skies and sunshine, then this wicked weather report might not be for you. It's about some of the wildest weather on the planet and the last places on Earth you'd pick to spend your summer hols in.

WICKED WEATHER RECORDS

1. Hottest place
Dallol, Ethiopia, is the hottest spot on Earth. The average temperature over a year is a scorching 34.4°C. But that's nothing compared to toasty Al' Aziziyah in Libya. On 13 September 1922, the temperature reached a sizzling 58°C – IN THE SHADE!

2. Coldest place

Wrap up warm if you're visiting Vostok in Antarctica. The temperature's usually around a f-f-freezing −57.8°C, and in 1983, it plummeted to a bone-chilling −89.2°C. By that time, you wouldn't be able to feel your fingers or toes. You'd probably have frozen to death.

3. Wettest place

The world's wettest place is soggy Mawsynram in India, where almost 12,000 mm of rain falls EVERY YEAR. You'll also need your brolly if you're visiting Mount Wai-'ale-'ale in Hawaii. Buckets of rain fall every day for as many as 350 days a year.

4. Driest place

Dying of thirst is a real danger in the desperate Atacama Desert in Chile. It's officially the driest place on Earth. For 400 years (between 1570–1971) no rain fell at all. Trouble is, when it rained, it poured, and poured, and poured, causing furious flooding.

5. Windiest place

Back in Antarctica, breezy Commonwealth Bay is the windiest place in the world. Here gales gust at 320 km/h – that's as fast as a racing car. But the ghastliest gust ever recorded roared around Mount Washington, USA at 371 km/h.

6. Snowiest place

The most snow to fall in a single year was at Mount Rainier, USA, from 1971–1972. Some 31,000 mm of snow fell – enough to reach a third of the way up the Statue of Liberty. We don't know how many snowballs that would have made.

Wicked weather phobias

Does the sound of thunder make your legs turn to jelly? Do you find lightning frightening? Do you feel sick at the sight of snow? Some people don't just feel a bit under the weather. They're absolutely SCARED STIFF! But which of these wicked weather phobias do you think might be true?

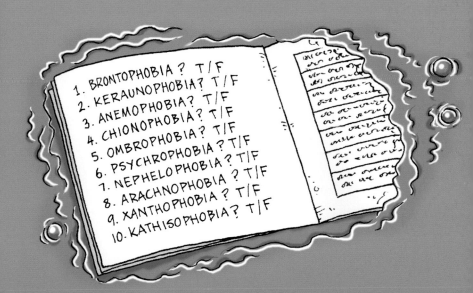

1. BRONTOPHOBIA ? T/F
2. KERAUNOPHOBIA? T/F
3. ANEMOPHOBIA? T/F
4. CHIONOPHOBIA? T/F
5. OMBROPHOBIA? T/F
6. PSYCHROPHOBIA? T/F
7. NEPHELOPHOBIA? T/F
8. ARACHNOPHOBIA ? T/F
9. XANTHOPHOBIA ? T/F
10. KATHISOPHOBIA? T/F

Answers:
1–7 ALL TRUE.
1 Brontophobia is the fear of thunder.
2 Keraunophobia is the fear of lightning.
3 Anemophobia is the fear of wind.
4 Chionophobia is the fear of snow.
5 Ombrophobia is the fear of rain.
6 Psychrophobia is the fear of cold.
7 Nephelophobia is the fear of clouds.

8–10 ALL FALSE.
8 Arachnophobia is the fear of spiders.
9 Xanthophobia is the fear of the colour yellow.
10 Kathisophobia is the fear of sitting down.

HORRIBLE HEALTH WARNING

If you're really keraunophobic or anemophobic, you might want to skip the rest of this book. If you're also kathisophobic, you might want to skip it standing up.

SHOCKING STORMS

It's one of the most dazzling sights in nature. The crash, bang, wallop of a thunderstorm. And with 1,800 thunderstorms rumbling away at any time of any day, chances are there's one set to brew near you soon. First, the sky turns black and brooding with towering thunderclouds. Then the sound and light show begins. A shocking flash of lightning is followed by a deafening crash of thunder. It's OK; you can take your fingers out of your ears now. I SAID... From the safety of your sofa, a storm might look a picture but you wouldn't want to get caught out in one. True, lightning can be horribly exciting but it's also a killer. Each year, in the USA alone, about 100 people are struck and killed. So what makes lightning so frightening? Why does thunder make such a din? And, more importantly, how on Earth do you weather a thunderstorm? Keep reading to find out the answer. This chapter is packed with horribly helpful hints and tips on how to survive.

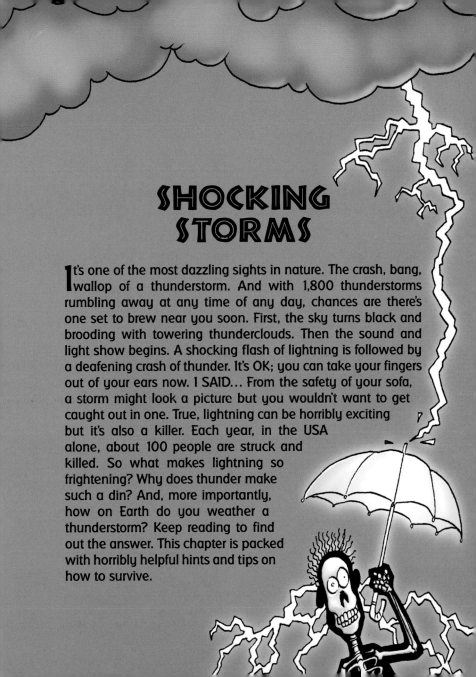

WICKED WEATHER REPORT

Name of weather: **LIGHTNING**
What it is: **A GIANT SPARK OF STATIC ELECTRICITY PRODUCED IN A THUNDERCLOUD**

HOW IT HAPPENS:

1 Air rushes up and down inside a thundercloud, making water droplets and ice particles inside the cloud collide.

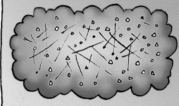

2 These collisions build up static electricity (that's the sort of electricity that makes your hair go crackly when you pull your jumper over your head).

3 Positive electrical charges build up in the top of the cloud. Negative charges build up in the bottom. The ground is positively charged.

4 When the pull becomes too strong, lightning flashes between the positive and negative charges.

LIGHTNING FACTS:

● Lightning finds the quickest route to the ground, so tall building and trees are top targets.

● A flash of lighting looks like it flickers but it doesn't really. It's because lightning's made up of lots of mini flashes that travel so quickly you can't see them separately.

● The lightning you see is the 'return' stroke from the ground to the cloud. The flash from the cloud to the ground is called the 'leader' stroke.

● About 100 flashes of lightning hit the Earth EVERY SINGLE SECOND.

Could you be a fulminologist*
* That's the posh name for a scientist who studies lightning.

Which of these five frightful thunderstorm facts is true?

1	Thunderstorms only happen in winter?	True	False
2	Lightning's five times hotter than the sun?	True	False
3	Thunder's the sound of clouds colliding?	True	False
4	Thunderstorms can trigger tornadoes?	True	False
5	Hail's another hazard of thunderstorms?	True	False

Answers:

1 FALSE. Thunderstorms usually happen in summer when the weather's warm and sticky. These make ideal conditions for a storm to start. As the Sun heats the Earth's surface, it warms the air, which starts to rise. As the warm air rises and cools, it condenses (some of the water vapour gas in it turns into liquid water), creating gigantic cumulonimbus clouds (thunder clouds). And it's in these monster clouds that thunderstorms are born.

2 TRUE. As a sizzling streak of lightning flashes across the sky, it can heat the air in its path to a scorching 33,000°C. That's about five times hotter than the surface of the Sun. How's that for hot stuff?

3 FALSE. For centuries, people hadn't the foggiest idea why thunder happened, so they made up stories about colliding clouds to explain what they heard. Other people thought thunder was made by a monster bird flapping its monster wings. But what really happens is this... As lighting heats up the air around it, the air expands at supersonic speed and this what makes the booming sound of thunder.

4 TRUE. Some awesome thunderstorms grow in rows called squall lines, with the strongest storms at the ends. These superstorms can last for several hours (a storm usually blows itself out in 30 minutes) and often bring a terrifying tornado or two along for company. (See page 25 for the low-down on tornadoes.)

5 TRUE. Just when you think the storm's blown over, it's got one more trick up its sleeve. A load of rock-hard hailstones comes crashing down on your head. Hailstones happen inside a thundercloud when ice crystals get tossed up and down. Water freezes on to the crystals in layers until they're heavy enough to fall as hail. Most hailstones are roughly pea-sized, but a whopping hailstone the size of a watermelon once fell in Kansas, USA. Ouch!

EARTH—SHATTERING FACT

American pilot, Lt Col William Rankin got the shock of his life when he was forced to bail out of his plane ... straight into a thundercloud. For 45 heart-stopping minutes, he was battered by howling, gale-force winds and drenched with rain until he thought he'd drown. Miraculously, his parachute wasn't damaged and, after his appalling ordeal, he eventually landed safely in a field. He hitched a lift to hospital, where he was treated for shock and frostbite – but he was lucky to be alive.

Six shocking lightning strikes

Athlone, Ireland, 1697

Sparks flew when a single bolt of lightning struck the castle's ammunition store and the 260 barrels of gunpowder and 1,000 hand grenades inside. The whole lot went up in smoke, blowing the castle and the nearby town to smithereens.

Virginia, USA, 1942–1976

Retired park ranger Roy C Sullivan proved lightning can strike twice. At least. Over 35 years, he was struck a shocking SEVEN times. Incredibly, Roy lived to tell the tale and suffered only minor injuries. He had his eyebrows scorched, his hair set on fire (twice), twisted his ankle and suffered various burns.

Chicago, USA, 1975

Top golfer Lee Trevino got a nasty shock when he was struck by lightning during a competition. He was sitting out a storm by the side of a lake, when lightning hit him and knocked him out. The lightning flashed off the lake, shot through his metal golf club and streaked up his back, but he wasn't badly hurt.

Karlskrone, Sweden, 1988

With wild weather on the way, a woman who was scared stiff of thunder ran out of her house and down the road to her neighbour's. Lightning struck the top of her umbrella and she fell to the ground, knocking all the fillings out of her teeth. Luckily, she was soon on the mend and on her way to see a dentist.

Virginia, USA, 1987

There were fireworks when a lightning strike triggered the launch of three space rockets ... AT THE SAME TIME. Two rockets shot over the sea while the other raced along the ground. Oddly, one of the rockets was packed with scientific instruments for measuring, er, lightning.

Durunka, Egypt, 1994

On 2 November, lightning struck a train carrying a cargo of fuel oil. The bolt blew the train off the track and it exploded with a massive bang. This sparked off a gigantic fireball that surged through the town, setting it on fire.

HORRIBLE HEALTH WARNING

Being struck by lightning can knock your socks off. And knock you off your feet. If you're lucky, you'll feel like you've been hit by a sledgehammer. If you're unlucky, you'll be dead. Even if you survive the shock, you'll probably have a s splitting headache, feel sick, hear ringing in your ears and find burn marks shaped like a spider's web all over your skin. And if that's not enough to cope with, you'll also have trouble remembering things.

Storm warning signs

Apart from colossal clouds, there are other clues that a storm's brewing. Here are some of the strangest signs to spot.

• *Bees flying back to their hives.*
It seems bees can detect changes in humidity (that's the amount of water vapour in the air). Humidity is high before a thunderstorm. Then the bad–tempered bees buzz off home. Mind you don't get stung.

• *Swallows flying high in the sky.*
Before a storm, the weather is horribly unsettled as warm air starts to rise. Insects get carried away on the rising air, and are blown up into the sky. The swallows follow closely behind – insects are their favourite food.

• *Your head starting to ache.*
Some people are seriously sensitive to the weather. They even claim they can feel the weather in their bones. Sounds painful. Others get headaches when the air's humid or sizzling with static electricity – the ideal conditions for a thunderstorm.

• *Your hair standing on end.*
Yep, some people find storms a hair-raising experience because of all the static electricity in the air. But by the time this happens, it may be too late to escape. A lightning strike may only be seconds away.

• *Thunder turning milk sour.*
OK, so this one's actually a fib, though people believed it for centuries. Milk goes sour if it gets warm and you often get warm weather before a thunderstorm. But this has nothing to do with thunder and it won't happen if you keep the milk in the fridge.

Ten ways to avoid being struck by lightning

Before a storm…

✓ DO keep an eye on the sky. Apart from bad-tempered bees, darkening skies and gusty winds are both signs a storm's brewing.

✓ DO find out how far away the storm is. Thunder and lightning happen at exactly the same time, but you see lightning before you hear thunder because light travels much faster than sound. Here's how you can work out if a storm's just around the corner:

a) When you see a flash of lightning, look at your watch.*

b) Count the seconds until you hear thunder.

c) Divide the number of seconds by three. That'll tell you how far away the storm is in kilometres.

d) If the distance is 10 km or less, you're at risk of being struck.

*(If you don't have a watch with a second hand, count the seconds like this 'One one thousand, two one thousand…' and so on.)

If you're indoors…

✗ **DON'T** use the phone. If lightning strikes, it could send a killer charge down the line. Steer clear of other electrical equipment like TVs and computers.

✗ **DON'T** have a bath or shower. Water is a brilliant conductor (something that's good at carrying electricity; metal's another one). Even doing the washing-up can be risky (so there's a good excuse).

If you're outside…

✓ **DO** get to shelter fast. This should be a building where lightning can flow through the electrical wiring and plumbing safely into the ground. Your house will bc, cr, safe as houses, but you'll fry in a flimsy shed or tent. Wait at least 30 minutes after the last strike to go outside again.

✓ **DO** stay in your car. But close the windows – lightning can sneak through the smallest cracks. And don't touch anything. The lightning should run around the car's metal body and away from you.

✗ **DON'T** stand under a tall tree. Lightning always takes the quickest path to the ground so trees, tall buildings, telephone poles and even hilltops are all at risk of being struck.

✓ **DO** crouch down on the ground. If you're caught out in the open, crouch down low with your feet together and your head tucked in. This'll make you less of a target. But don't lie down – the ground might be wet.

ACTUALLY, I DON'T THINK THAT *WAS* LIGHTNING!

✓ DO keep your distance. If you're with other people, spread out and stay apart. Then, if lightning strikes one of you, it won't zap the others as well.

✗ DON'T go swimming. You'll be a sitting duck. And avoid going fishing or playing golf. Metal golf clubs and carbon-fibre fishing rods are excellent conductors, and the fish might not be the only things that get fried.

EARTH—SHATTERING FACT

Long ago, people thought they could scare off lightning by ringing the church bells. Big mistake. Many barmy bell-ringers ended up as toast when lightning struck the tall church steeples and zapped the metal bells. Other people thought carrying an acorn about would stop them getting fried. Nuts.

TWISTED TORNADOES

It's one thing finding a breeze bracing or liking the feel of the wind in your face. But the winds you'll meet in this chapter aren't the sort that rustle leaves or cool you down on a hot day. These wild winds can lift up a train from its tracks and blow your house to smithereens. Meet a tornado! Get mixed up with a terrifying tornado and you'll know what it means to be blown away. It'll suck you up, spit you out, and you won't have time to call for help. The best way to survive a tornado is to GET OUT OF ITS WAY! Trouble is, you can never tell exactly where a tornado will strike next. So if one starts to twist near you, here are some life-saving tips to make your head spin…

WICKED WEATHER REPORT

Name of weather: TORNADO
What it is: A VIOLENT FUNNEL-SHAPED STORM THAT SPINS DOWN FROM A THUNDERCLOUD

HOW IT HAPPENS:

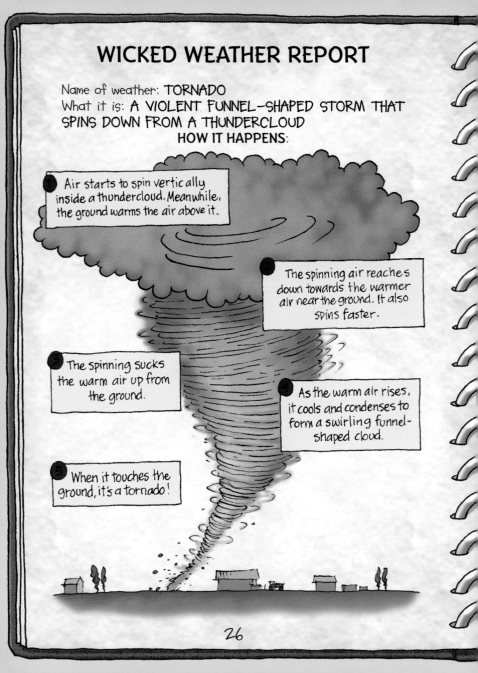

1. Air starts to spin vertically inside a thundercloud. Meanwhile, the ground warms the air above it.

2. The spinning air reaches down towards the warmer air near the ground. It also spins faster.

3. The spinning sucks the warm air up from the ground.

4. As the warm air rises, it cools and condenses to form a swirling funnel-shaped cloud.

5. When it touches the ground, it's a tornado!

TORNADO FACTS:

● Tornadoes usually happen in the afternoon or early evening. That's when thunderstorms are most likely. But not always. The deadliest twisters strike at night when their victims are fast asleep.

● Tornadoes have stormed across every continent ... except icy Antarctica.

● North of the equator, tornadoes twist anti-clockwise. South of the equator, it's clockwise.

● Waterspouts are tornadoes that twist over the sea and can be over a kilometre tall. No wonder worried ancient sailors mistook them for sea monsters.

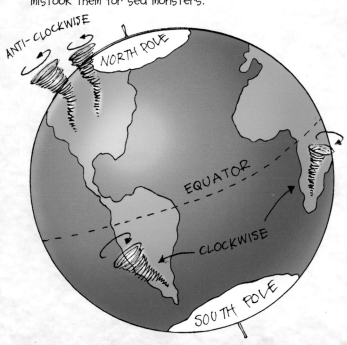

HORRIBLE HEALTH WARNING

If you're planning your summer holidays, you might want to give Tornado Alley a wide berth. It's a stretch of the USA from Texas through Oklahoma, Kansas, Nebraska and the Dakotas. And it's home to the wildest winds on Earth. A terrifying 700 tornadoes rip through every year, mostly in spring and early summer.

Six twisted tornado questions

Q 1: How big is a tornado?

A: Monster twisters can grow up to a kilometre wide but they're usually much smaller than that. Some titchy tornadoes are only a few metres across. But small can be deadly and these beauties pack a powerful punch.

Q 2: How fast do tornadoes blow?

A: The winds inside a tornado are the strongest on Earth. They're horribly tricky to measure but experts reckon they can reach speeds of up to 480 km/h. The strongest winds are right in the centre of the tornado, close to the ground.

Q 3: How fast do tornadoes travel?

A: It depends. They usually zip along at about 55 km/h – that's about ten times as fast as you can walk. But some can really move. The fastest tornado ever reached an awesome 120 km/h – you'd never keep up with that.

Q 4: How long do they last?

A: Tornadoes can last anything from a minute or two to several hours. The longest ever recorded was an incredible 7.5 hours long. Once a twister runs out of warm air and energy, it starts to collapse. The funnel looks like a twisted rope, then finally dies away.

Q 5: What happens when tornadoes touch down?

A: Tornadoes hit the ground running and smash everything in their path. And they pick up bits of flying debris and turn them into deadly weapons. A tornado's trail of destruction can be from a few metres to a few hundred kilometres wide. And it can tear along for as much as 350 km before it finally runs out of steam.

Q 6: What colour are tornadoes?

A: Most tornadoes are grey or black from all the dust and dirt they suck up from the ground. But a tornado that tore through the USA in 1991 was a pretty shade of pink from the thousands of geranium petals it sucked up when it ripped apart a greenhouse.

HOW TO MEASURE A TORNADO

It's horribly hard to measure a tornado because the winds inside are so wild they'd smash any weather instruments into matchsticks. So experts look at the chaos they cause when they touch down. Then they guess the wind speed and grade the tornado on the horribly handy **Enhanced Fujita Scale**.

SCALE	WIND SPEED	TYPE OF DAMAGE

SCALE   **WIND SPEED**   **TYPE OF DAMAGE**

EF0   105–137km/h   **Light damage.**

Lifts off some roof tiles; breaks off branches; pushes over small trees.

EF1   138–178km/h   **Moderate damage.**

Strips off roofs; breaks off doors; smashes windows.

EF2   179–218km/h   **Considerable damage.**

Rips off roofs; smashes mobile homes; snaps large trees; lifts cars off ground.

EF3   219–266km/h   **Severe damage.**

Destroys whole houses; derails trains; lifts and throws cars into air; blows away flimsy buildings.

EF4   267–322 km/h   **Devastating damage.**

Flattens houses and shopping malls; hurls cars and other missiles.

EF5   Over 322km/h   **Incredible damage.**

Sweeps away houses; hurls cars hundreds of metres through air; damages high-rise buildings.

Answers:

Believe it or not, they're all TRUE!

a) In 2001, a pet rabbit called Houdini had a lucky escape after his hutch was sucked into air by a tornado in Norfolk, England. The wind hurled the hutch over a 2-metre-high fence before sending it crashing into a meadow. Houdini was later found sitting next to his wrecked home, hopping mad but unharmed.

b) Never mind 'rock-a-bye baby'. In 1981, a tornado swept through the city of Ancona in Italy and sucked up a pram with a baby asleep inside. Then it plonked the pram down again on the ground. Astonishingly, the baby didn't notice a thing.

c) When a tornado starts running out of energy, it may spit out a surprise or two. Like the alligator that fell from the sky in South Carolina, USA, in 1843. And that's not all. Apart from alarmed alligators, tornadoes have also dumped bucketloads of fish, frogs, mice, crabs, starfish and even whole flocks of geese.

d) A 350-tonne train travelling through Minnesota, USA in 1931 was lifted clean off its tracks by a tornado. Then the bad-tempered twister dumped it in a nearby ditch. Incredibly, only one of the passengers was killed.

e) In June 1953, a woman in Massachusetts, USA, found a wedding dress in her back garden. It was dirty and crumpled but otherwise good as new. She traced it back to a woman who lived 70 km away. A tornado had blown the dress out of her house. Talk about a whirlwind romance.

A twisted tale

McKinney, Texas, USA, May 1943

Tornadoes strike with such fury survivors can't remember what hit them. Usually. But on 3 May 1943, retired farmer, Roy S Hall, not only came face to face with a tornado but also lived to describe his terrifying ordeal.

When a tornado screeched towards his home, Hall, his wife and four children rushed into a bedroom for safety. Seconds later, the outside wall caved in with a colossal crash. The family's petrifying experience had begun. Suddenly, everything went quiet. Hall said it was 'exactly as if hands had been placed over my ears, cutting off all sound.' In the eerie silence, a strange, blue glow lit up the house. Just then, Hall was tossed through the air and buried under a pile of rubble. He clawed his way out, grabbed his four-year-old daughter and waited for his house to blow away. Then he saw a terrible sight…

Something had billowed down from above him and was hovering around him, almost motionless. Then Hall realized where he was – trapped right inside a tornado's funnel! Looking up, he saw a shiny wall of cloud. It was like being inside a giant drainpipe, he said later. The funnel reached up for hundreds of metres and swayed gently from side to side. As it swayed, it seemed to be made from a stack of huge rippling rings.

34

Horrified, Hall watched the funnel tip over and smash his neighbour's house to pieces. He was sure he and his family were about to die. Then, unbelievably, the tornado turned tail and sped away. The Hall family had had an amazingly lucky escape. Their house lay in ruins but, apart from a few bruises, they were unharmed.

Five terrible twisters

Missouri, Illinois, Indiana, USA, 1925

The USA's worst tornado disaster was the Tri-State tornado of 1925. On 18 March, this violent EF5 twister roared across the three states of Missouri, Illinois and Indiana, killing 695 people and injuring thousands more. The tornado lasted for 3.5 hours and blasted a terrible trail of destruction over 350 km long.

Bulahdelah, Australia, 1970

Australia's most destructive tornado passed near the small coastal town of Bulahdelah on 1 January. At least EF4 in strength, it ripped a path over 20 km long and 1.6 km wide through the state forest. Fortunately, nobody lived nearby so there weren't any casualties. But the tornado destroyed more than a million trees and tossed a two-tonne tractor into the air.

USA and southern Canada, 1974

On 3–4 April, a staggering 148 tornadoes slammed into 13 states of the USA, and parts of southern Canada. This so-called 'Super Tornado Outbreak' lasted for 18 horrific hours and six of the tornadoes reached a violent EF5. Tragically, 315 people were killed and over 5,000 injured. But things could have been a whole lot worse if the warning system hadn't worked so well.

Dhaka, Bangladesh, 1989

The deadliest twister ever struck near Dhaka in Bangladesh on 26 April. This dreadful disaster claimed at least 1,300 lives, injured about 12,000 and left 100,000 people homeless. It struck in the evening, when most people were at home. Unfortunately. Some 90 per cent of homes were flattened in over 150 villages and farmers' crops were ruined.

Birmingham, England, 2005

A tornado that hit the city of Birmingham on 28 July touched down for just four minutes. In that time it managed to damage 1,000 houses, uproot trees and injure 22 people. Britain has about 40 tornadoes a year, though they're mostly pretty paltry compared to the real giants. Tornadoes as big as the Birmingham twister strike about once every two years. But they usually crash through the countryside without doing much damage.

Tornado warning signs

Despite having loads of high-tech gear, experts can't tell exactly where a tornado will strike next, but there are some tell-tale signs they look out for. Trouble is, some tornadoes strike without any warning at all.

Bulging thundercloud

A thundercloud's top is usually flat, unless a tornado's brewing. Then the air near the centre rushes up and punches a hole in the top.

Udder-shaped clouds

Drooping clouds hanging down from under a thundercloud are signs of seriously stormy weather. Some people say these clouds look a bit like a cow's udders.

IT'S GLOOMY UDDER HERE!

Dark green sky

The sky often turns darkish-green when hail's on its way. And hail only happens in thunderstorms where a tornado or two might be brewing.

GREEN SKY AT NIGHT, SHEPHERDS RUN FOR COVER!

Loud roaring sound

People who've survived a tornado say they heard a loud, roaring sound like a jet engine or a train. And they knew it was time to get outta there – fast.

EARTH—SHATTERING FACT

The best way to track a tornado is by horribly high-tech Doppler radar. Hail, heavy rain and high winds show up on a screen to tell you which way the tornado's heading. Trouble is, even this red-hot radar can't tell you if a tornado's touched down. So in the USA, thousands of eagle-eyed people are trained as storm spotters. They keep their eyes peeled on the sky to spot the signs that a tornado is on the way. Fancy a job?

HOW'S THE DOPPLER GOING?

TORNADO SAFETY – SURVIVAL TIPS

1 Head for your storm shelter. If you've got one. This is an underground shelter in the cellar or outside the house that's common in places prone to tornadoes.

2 Get into the bath. If you don't have a storm shelter, don't panic. Go to the basement or the lowest part of the building. Or head for an inside room with no windows, like a bathroom or under the stairs. Get into the bath or hide under a mattress.

3 Stay away from windows. The worse place to be is a room with lots of windows or outside walls. The tornado will simply smash them to pieces and turn the glass and bricks into deadly flying missiles.

4 Pack a survival kit. You'll need drinking water, tinned food, a change of clothes, a blanket or sleeping bag and a first-aid kit. A torch (with spare batteries) and a battery-powered radio for listening to weather forecasts is a must.

5 Hide in a ditch. If you're caught outside and you can't get to shelter, find a ditch or lie down flat on the ground. Cover your head with your hands. High winds and flying debris should pass over you. But mind the ditch doesn't flood.

6 Get out of your car. Never try to sit out a tornado in your car. Tornadoes can lug heavyweight trains around so your car would be seriously small fry. You could easily be blown off the road, or picked up and hurled about.

7 Keep away from bridges. Sheltering under a bridge might seem safe but it isn't. The shape of the bridge might whip the winds up even more, causing the bridge to collapse or blasting you with flying debris.

8 Practise a tornado drill. It's a bit like the fire drill you practise at school. And it could save your life. You need to work out exactly what to do if a tornado strikes, where to go for shelter, and what to do if you get split up from your family or friends.

DON'T PANIC!

I'VE ONLY JUST WASHED THIS!

HORRIBLE HURRICANES

What do hurricanes, typhoons, cyclones and willy-willies have in common? They're all names for furiously spinning storms, that's what, just in different parts of the world. They rage across tropical oceans but woe betide you when they hit land. If you thought thunderstorms and tornadoes were horribly dangerous, you ain't seen nothing yet. Hair-raising hurricanes are the DEADLIEST STORMS ON THE PLANET. This is seriously wicked weather and if you get in the way of a hurricane, you'll be lucky to be alive. But it's not all doom and gloom. If you get to know how a hurricane blows, you might just be able to stay one step ahead. Ready for a whirlwind tour?

WICKED WEATHER REPORT

Type of weather: HURRICANE
What it is: GIGANTIC, SPINNING STORM

HOW IT HAPPENS:

5 MORE WARM, MOIST AIR RISES, MAKING THE STORM SPIN FASTER. WHEN THE WINDS REACH 118 km/h, IT'S OFFICIALLY A HURRICANE!

4 THE EARTH'S ROTATION MAKES THE RISING AIR TWIST AROUND A CENTRE AND THE STORM STARTS TO SPIN...

3 AS THE AIR RISES, IT COOLS DOWN AND CONDENSES TO MAKE TOWERING THUNDER-CLOUDS AND RAIN...

2 THE WARM AIR HOLDS LOTS OF WATER VAPOUR WHICH EVAPORATES* FROM THE SURFACE OF THE SEA. THIS WARM AIR RISES QUICKLY...

1 HURRICANES HAPPEN OVER WARM, TROPICAL SEAS. THE WARM SEA HEATS THE AIR ABOVE IT...

* EVAPORATION'S WHEN WATER'S WARMED UP AND TURNS FROM LIQUID INTO WATER-VAPOUR GAS

HURRICANE FACTS
- The sea temperature must be at least 27°C for a hurricane to grow.
- There are hundreds of tropical storms each year but only about 35 reach full hurricane force. Phew!
- Seedlings are small clusters of thunderstorms that 'bloom' into hurricanes.
- A hurricane sucks up about 2 billion tonnes of moisture a day through evaporation from the sea.

THIS IS THE LAST STRAW!

SLURP!

SEA

HORRIBLE HEALTH WARNING
To avoid being hit by a hurricane, steer clear of the Atlantic Ocean from 1 June to 30 November. That's when the sea is at exactly the right toasty temperature for hurricanes to form. Early September is especially hurricane-prone. Bad news if you're heading for the Pacific Ocean – it's hurricane season all year round there.

FIVE HAIR-RAISING FACTS ABOUT HURRICANES

1 They're huge.

An average-sized hurricane is about 480 km wide, but a real giant could reach 960 km and tower more than 8 km tall.

2 They've got eyes.

The eye is the circular centre of the hurricane where the wind drops and the sky's clear and blue. Unlike the wicked weather raging all around. The eye is about 30–65 km across. It's surrounded by a ring of towering thunderclouds, called the eyewall.

3 They're fast.

To count as a hurricane, winds must be blowing at 118 km/h, but they can howl much harder than that. In a fully blown hurricane, winds can roar along as fast an express train. The strongest winds are in the eyewall.

4 They're bursting with energy.

If you could turn all the energy from a hurricane into electricity, you'd have enough to power the whole of the USA for THREE YEARS! Trouble is, no one's worked out a way of collecting all this energy.

5 They run out of energy when they hit land.

Hurricanes get their energy from the warm, moist air they suck up from the sea. So once they hit land, their supply is switched off. They gradually get weaker – but not before they've caused chaos.

How to measure a hurricane

Hurricanes are measured according to how strongly they're blowing and how much damage they cause when they hit land. Then they're graded from one to five on the Saffir-Simpson hurricane scale. Category 1 is the weakest, but get up to Category 5 and you're talking full-scale catastrophe.

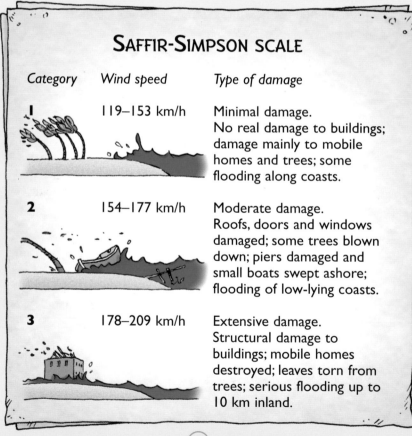

SAFFIR-SIMPSON SCALE

Category	Wind speed	Type of damage
1	119–153 km/h	Minimal damage. No real damage to buildings; damage mainly to mobile homes and trees; some flooding along coasts.
2	154–177 km/h	Moderate damage. Roofs, doors and windows damaged; some trees blown down; piers damaged and small boats swept ashore; flooding of low-lying coasts.
3	178–209 km/h	Extensive damage. Structural damage to buildings; mobile homes destroyed; leaves torn from trees; serious flooding up to 10 km inland.

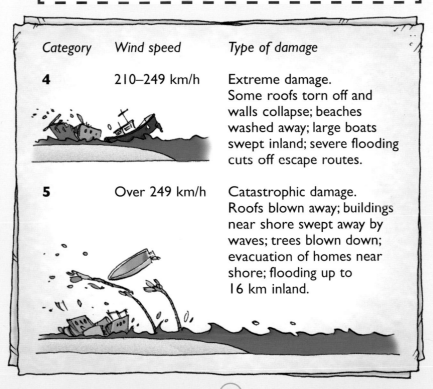

Category	Wind speed	Type of damage
4	210–249 km/h	Extreme damage. Some roofs torn off and walls collapse; beaches washed away; large boats swept inland; severe flooding cuts off escape routes.
5	Over 249 km/h	Catastrophic damage. Roofs blown away; buildings near shore swept away by waves; trees blown down; evacuation of homes near shore; flooding up to 16 km inland.

What's in a name?
Hurricanes were first given names in the 19th century by Australian weatherman Clement Wragge. He named them after politicians he'd got it in for. Today, names are taken from a list, drawn up in alphabetical order. A new list is made every year.

ATLANTIC OCEAN HURRICANE NAMES

2008	2009	2010
Arthur	Ana	Alex
Bertha	Bill	Bonnie
Cristobal	Claudette	Colin
Dolly	Danny	Danielle
Edouard	Erika	Earl
Fay	Fred	Fiona
Gustav	Grace	Gaston
Hanna	Henri	Hermine
Ike	Ida	Igor
Josephine	Joaquin	Julia
Kyle	Kate	Karl
Laura	Larry	Lisa
Marco	Mindy	Matthew
Nana	Nicholas	Nicole
Omar	Odette	Otto
Paloma	Peter	Paula
Rene	Rose	Richard
Sally	Sam	Shary
Teddy	Teresa	Tomas
Vicky	Victor	Virginie
Wilfred	Wanda	Walter

THAT'S A BIG GUSTAV WIND!

Deadly durian triggers mudslides
Philippines, December 2006

Thousands of people were killed or went missing as Typhoon Durian slammed into the Philippines at the beginning of December 2006. A seriously wild Category-4 storm, it unleashed winds howling at around 250 km/h, together with torrential rain.

The typhoon left a trail of devastation across the islands. Worst hit were villages on the slopes of Mount Mayon, an active volcano. Driving rain sent murderous mudslides crashing down the volcano's slopes, burying whole villages and their inhabitants in suffocating, black sludge. The village of Pedang at the foot of the volcano was particularly badly hit. The mudslides hit with such force, victims had their clothes ripped off as they were swept away.

Rescue workers struggled with the grim task of pulling bodies out of the mud with their bare hands. No one was found alive, although some people were rescued from the rooftops of their homes, which poked out above the mud. One man, Glen Lorica, told rescuers how a torrent of mud uprooted trees and rocks swept his home away. He managed to stay afloat by grabbing hold of a tree but he was badly battered by huge boulders and other debris. His sister also survived the appalling ordeal but the rest of their family was still missing. The people of the Philippines had been unlucky. Dead unlucky. Durian was the fourth typhoon to strike the region in just three months. And no sooner had it ended, than another mega-storm, Typhoon Utor, roared in.

HURRICANE ROGUES GALLERY

Name: Hurricane Camille
Date: August 1969
Hardest hit: Mississippi, Louisiana, Virginia, USA
Maximum wind speed: 305 km/h
Rating: Category 5
Damage:
● Camille caused 260 deaths, injured over 8,000 people and flattened thousands of homes.
● A massive storm surge left the Mississippi shoreline completely destroyed.
● Only one guest survived a 'hurricane party' held at Pass Christian, Mississippi ... where Camille made landfall.

Name: Bhola cyclone
Date: November 1970
Hardest hit: Bangladesh
Maximum wind speed: 185 km/h
Rating: Category 3
Damage:
● It was the deadliest cyclone on record with over 300,000 deaths, including 46,000 fishermen.
● Most deaths were caused when storm surge flooded the low-lying islands of the Ganges River delta.
● The region's storm-warning system wasn't working properly, so many people didn't even realize a cyclone was coming.

Name: Cyclone Tracy
Date: December 1974
Hardest hit: Darwin, Australia
Maximum wind speed: 217 km/h
Rating: Category 4
Damage:

- Tracy slammed into Darwin on Christmas Day, taking the city by surprise. It was supposed to pass by safely many kilometres to the north.
- Tracy was the smallest cyclone on record. Small but deadly.
- Over two thirds of the city's buildings were destroyed. The city later had to be completely rebuilt, using modern storm-proof building materials.

Name: Hurricane Gilbert
Date: September 1988
Hardest hit: Jamaica
Maximum wind speed: 320 km/h
Rating: Category 5
Damage:

- The most violent hurricane to hit Jamaica for over 30 years.
- In Jamaica, Gilbert caused over $10 billion of damage, destroying crops, buildings – including all but two of the island's hospitals – and roads.
- Gilbert's rain zone stretched 1,000 km from its centre. It chucked down over 700 mm of rain, causing fatal flash flooding in the mountains.

Name: Hurricane Mitch
Date: October/November 1998
Hardest hit: Honduras, Nicaragua
Maximum wind speed: 290 km/h
Rating: Category 5
Damage:
- Mitch killed more than 11,000 people with as many again missing.
- Worst hit was Honduras, where two thirds of crops were ruined and whole areas wiped off the map.
- Record rainfall caused murderous mudslides that buried people alive. Two thirds of Honduras's bridges and roads were washed away.

HORRIBLE HEALTH WARNING

The names of especially deadly hurricanes are 'retired' and never used again. So it's goodbye Durian, Camille, Gilbert and Mitch. And so long Katrina, Anita, Celia, David, Andrew and George, to name just a few.

WE HAVEN'T QUITE DECIDED ON A NAME FOR THE HURRICANE JUST YET...

EARL!

LISA!

Five ways of halting a hurricane

Chuck chemicals in it

In the 1960s, American scientists tried to halve a hurricane's power by dropping a chemical called silver iodide into it. They reckoned this would make the eyewall bigger and slow the winds down. And at first, their potty plan seemed to work when it weakened Hurricane Debbie by a third. Trouble is, it also seemed to mess up rainfall patterns in other parts of the world.

Bomb it

Another idea was to blast the hurricane apart with nuclear weapons. But it's not as easy as it sounds. For a start, you'd need to explode a 10-megaton bomb EVERY 20 MINUTES just to match the hurricane's strength. And the blast would produce deadly radioactive fall-out that the wind would carry far and wide.

Seal the sea

Hurricanes are fuelled by huge amounts of water vapour that evaporates from the sea. So if you sealed the sea with some sort of liquid, you'd stop evaporation and hurricanes happening. Wouldn't you? Well, you might … if you could invent a liquid that wouldn't break up when you poured it on the choppy, storm-tossed sea.

Turn it to jelly

Dyn-O-Gel is a special powder that soaks up water and then turns into a gooey jelly. So you could chuck it into a hurricane to soak up the moisture that makes clouds and rain. Simple as that. There's just one teeny snag. You'd need a gigantic 37,000 tonnes of gel to gunk a hurricane – that's about 400 plane-loads. On the hour, every hour!

Cool the sea

Hurricanes get their energy from warm sea water, so cool the sea down and they'll soon fizzle out. All you'd need to do is tow some icebergs from the Arctic to the tropics, or pipe cold water up from the bottom of the sea. But again, size is the problem. You'd need an awful lot of icebergs or pipes to cool a hurricane-sized stretch of sea. And what if the tugboats got stuck in the storm?

ARE YOU SURE THIS'LL WORK...?

HORRIBLE HEALTH WARNING

Before you get too excited, NONE OF THESE IDEAS ARE LIKELY TO WORK! Most of them haven't even been tried. No one's managed to halt a hurricane ... yet. They're just too bloomin' big and unpredictable. And you might be in for a long wait. Your best bet for sitting the storm out is to learn to live with them by following our top survival tips.

HURRICANE SURVIVAL QUIZ

1 What does a hurricane watch mean?
a) A hurricane's likely in the next 24 hours.
b) A hurricane's likely in the next 36 hours.
c) A hurricane's likely but no one knows when.

2 What should you pack in your survival kit?
a) Drinking water.
b) Spare batteries.
c) Tinned food.

3 How should you hurricane-proof your house?
a) Tape up the windows.
b) Open the windows.
c) Board the windows up.

4 What should you do as the eye of the storm passes over?
a) Go outside to inspect the damage.
b) Stay indoors.
c) Take your storm shutters down.

5 Which side-effects should you avoid at all costs?
a) Storm surge.
b) Tornado.
c) Flash flood.

6 Where's the best place to shelter from the storm?
a) In a hurricane shelter.
b) Up a tree.
c) In a car.

Answers:

1 b) A hurricane watch means hurricane-force winds, heavy rain and flooding are possible in the next 36 hours. Stay tuned to your radio or TV for forecasts and orders to evacuate if necessary. If a hurricane's likely in the next 24 hours, a hurricane warning will be given. Then it's time to stay put in a safe shelter until the hurricane's passed.

2 a), b) & c) It's likely the electricity will get cut off, so you'll need spare batteries for your radio and torch. Don't use candles. If there's a gas leak, you'll go up with a bang. Take plenty of drinking water, in case the water supply's damaged. Store it in plastic bottles that won't break. Don't drink water from the tap during or after a hurricane, it may be contaminated. Tinned food that doesn't need cooking is a must while you sit out the storm. Pick food that won't go off. And don't forget to pack a can opener. You'll also need loads of other stuff, like clothes, medicines and a first-aid kit.

3 c) To stop your windows getting smashed by flying debris, you'll need to board them up. You can buy metal storm shutters that stay in place all the time. Or you can nail on planks of plywood but you'll need to do this well before the hurricane's due. Taping the windows won't stop the glass getting broken, and opening them will simply let the wind in.

4 b) As the eyes passes overhead, there's a short lull in the storm. But don't be tempted to rush out to look, whatever you do. It's only the calm before the other half of the storm.

The worst of the weather is probably still to come. Wait for the official 'all-clear' before going outside.

5 a) All three are side-effects of hurricanes and can be deadly. But nine out of ten people who die in hurricanes are killed by storm surges. What happens is this. The sea beneath the hurricane bulges. Then the wind blasts the bulge along, until it crashes on to the coast. When Hurricane Katrina hit the Gulf Coast of the USA in 2005, it triggered a storm surge 9 metres high. The water smashed through New Orleans' flood defences, flooding 80 per cent of the city, killing and injuring thousands of people.

6 a) Hurricane shelters are usually set up in public places like schools, churches or sports halls. Make sure you know where your nearest one is and the quickest way of getting to it. Then stay put until the storm's really over. If you're caught in a storm surge, climbing a tree is OK as a last resort. Sit as high up as possible, on the opposite side to the wind. Then sit tight and hope for the best. Never try to sit out a hurricane in your car – it won't stand a chance against wicked winds and flooding.

FATAL
FLOODS

Forget hair-raising hurricanes and terrifying tornadoes. Forget rumbling thunderstorms. The most dangerous kind of weather is … a fatal flood. Over the last 100 years, killer floods have claimed millions of lives – more than any other kind of wicked weather. Believe it or not. And it's all down to rain. Rain can be horribly useful. A quick shower can be refreshing, and plants and crops need rain to grow. Trouble is, 'it never rains but it pours', as the old saying goes. Too much rain and a slow-flowing river can turn into a raging torrent and flood the land all around. Worried about keeping your head above water? Don't panic. This chapter is packed with watertight tips if you're thrown in at the deep end.

I CAN'T SEE WHAT ALL THE FUSS IS ABOUT!

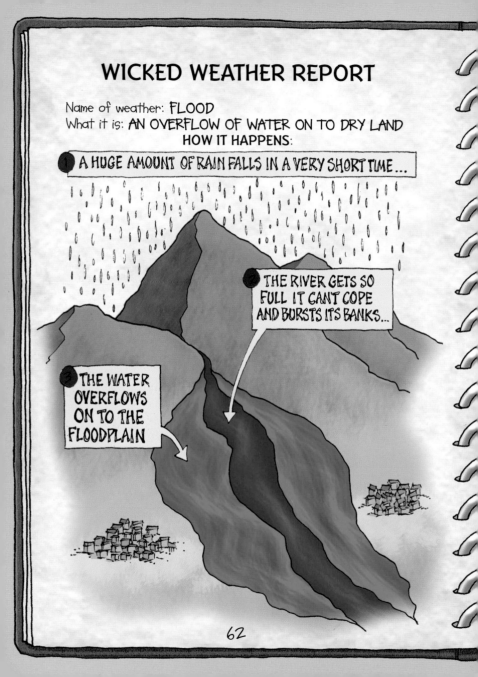

FLOOD FACTS:

- Floods also happen along the coast when tsunamis and hurricane storm—surges sweep ashore.
- Ice can make rivers overflow. Large chunks of ice can pile up if a river hits a bend, and clog it up.
- Dams designed to stop flooding (see page 73) can sometimes trigger deadly floods when they break or burst.
- A furious flood can be a killer, washing away buildings, bridges, roads, crops, animals ... and people.

WATER LEVEL

DAM

RIVER

HORRIBLE HEALTH WARNING

The deadliest kinds of floods are flash floods because they happen, er, in a flash. They're caused by sudden bursts of heavy rainfall, often from thunderstorms. And the reason they can be killers is because they strike so quickly and because they're horribly tricky to predict. If you're lucky, you'll have half an hour's warning. If you're unlucky, you'll get none at all.

EARTH-SHATTERING FACT

Horrible hydrologists (that's the posh name for scientists who study floods) rate floods by how frequent they are. And, oddly, the more often they happen, the better. A one-year flood is likely to strike once a year and won't do much damage. But a ten-year flood has a one-in-ten chance of happening in a year, and is far more serious. And the further you go up the scale, the worse it gets until you're in very deep water indeed. Imagine being hit by a 10,000-year flood. Of course, you can't. If you were really hit by a 10,000-year flood, you'd be swept away before you knew what was happening.

I WAITED 10,000 YEARS FOR *THIS*?

Eight killer floods

Huang He, China, 1931

The worst flood on record happened in 1931 when the Huang He (Yellow River) in China burst its banks. The flood lasted from July to November and left 4 million people dead. Some were drowned; others died in the famine that followed the flood. Another 80 million became homeless as the water soaked a staggering 88,400 square km of land. That's about the same size as Austria. One reason for the flooding is the massive amount of yellow mud the river lugs along. The mud blocks the smooth flow of the water and forces it to change its course.

Lynmouth, England, 1952

Never mind one-year floods. Or ten-year. Or even 10,000-year. In 1952, the little village of Lynmouth in England was smashed to pieces by a freak 50,000-YEAR FLOOD! The village sits in a valley where the River Lyn meets the sea. On 15 and 16 August, a storm dumped record amounts of rain. The overloaded river couldn't cope and cascaded through the town. Overnight, 34 people were killed and 100 houses destroyed. Some 132 cars were swept out to sea and debris littered the beach for miles. Among this were 15-tonne boulders that the raging river had swept along.

Florence, Italy, 1966

In November, in one of the worst storms in Italy's history, a two-day downpour hit the city of Florence. The River Arno flooded the city, cutting off electricity and breaking open oil tanks. Worse still, the city's sewers overflowed and stinking sewage poured out on to the streets. In places, the dirty water reached 6 metres deep, trapping people on the top floors of buildings. And worse was to come. When, at last, the water went down, the city lay under a thick carpet of oily water and foul-smelling slime. Many beautiful buildings were damaged and priceless works of art ruined.

Brisbane, Australia, 1974

Over much of Australia, it doesn't rain very often and rain's a precious resource. But in 1974, Cyclone Wanda passed close by, triggering three weeks of heavy rainfall over the state of Queensland. By late January, every river was in flood. Around the city of Brisbane, the flood caused an estimated $200 million and killed 14 people. At least 6,700 homes were flooded and some houses were completely washed away. At the height of the flood, a massive oil tanker was torn from its mooring in the river and set adrift. It was the worst flooding an Australian city had ever known.

Colorado, USA, 1976

On 31 July, a thunderstorm dumped a year's rainfall into Big Thompson River ... *IN LESS THAN FIVE HOURS!* It turned the usually shallow, slow-moving river into a raging torrent. That evening, a wall of water more than 6 metres deep, roared down the canyon. The flood happened so quickly that there wasn't time to issue a warning. Some 140 people, mostly campers, were killed and hundreds more were injured. And 400 cars, 418 houses and most of Route 34 were washed away. Luckily, another flood this fierce doesn't look likely for a few thousand years.

Mississippi River, USA, 1993

Along the Mississippi River, floods are a fact of life. And, with new flood-proof measures in place, really big floods seemed a thing of the past. But months of record rainfall changed all that. The swollen river roared along at six times its usual rate. By the time the water went down in October, it had flooded an area twice the size of Sweden, destroyed 43,000 homes and left 70,000 people homeless. Enormous amounts of mud and sand were dumped on nearby farmland, ruining the year's harvest. Several towns were relocated to higher ground. As for the flood-proof measures, they didn't stand a chance.

Mozambique, Africa, 2000

Five weeks of heavy rain in February and March caused rivers in Mozambique to burst their banks. The catastrophic flooding that followed was made worse when Cyclone Eline hit. Tragically, about 800 people were killed and about 25,000 made homeless. Crops, cattle, roads and bridges were drowned or washed away. One of the luckiest flood survivors was a baby born in a tree. His mother had managed to climb up to escape the flood water. Both mother and baby were later rescued by helicopter and taken to hospital.

Mumbai, India, 2005

In July, India's largest city, Mumbai, was bombarded by the worst monsoon rains on record. A staggering 940 mm of water fell in just one day, bringing the city to a standstill. As the transport system collapsed, there was chaos on the streets as people tried to wade home. More than 1,000 people drowned or were killed by landslides or collapsing buildings. Others died from diseases caught from dirty water supplies. Experts put part of the blame for the disaster on the fact that many of the city's drains were clogged up with chucked-out plastic bags.

EARTH-SHATTERING FACT

Despite the danger, thousands of people all over the world live in places likely to flood. So why on Earth do they give it a go? Well, floodplains are brilliant for growing bumper crops on. When rivers flood, they dump thick, gooey black mud on the floodplains and this mud is rich in the minerals plants need to grow. Every flood brings a fresh supply. But it's a horribly risky lifestyle because a really fierce flood can wash away a whole year's crops.

FATAL FLOOD ACTION GUIDE

BEFORE...

Listen out for flood warnings. You might hear them on the radio or TV. Some places sound a siren if time's short. Make sure you know what the warnings mean:

a) Flood watch: flooding's likely on low-lying land and roads.

b) Flood warning: flooding's expected. Get ready to move.

c) Serious flood warning: serious flooding's expected and you're in danger.

Have some sandbags handy. You'll need them to block up airbricks and doorways. Pile them up in a pyramid shape. Put an extra sandbag in the toilet to stop smelly sewage flowing up.

Make a flood kit. You'll need a torch, batteries, portable radio, blankets, waterproof clothing, wellies and a first-aid kit. Stock up on plastic bags to put any valuables and important documents in. Try to keep the kit upstairs out of the way of the water.

Turn off the gas and electricity. Water and electricity don't mix. Water is a top conductor of electricity (that means electricity can zap through it easily). Touch electrical equipment with wet hands and you could be in for a nasty shock.

DURING...

Get ready to evacuate. If the flood's really bad, you might have to leave home ... fast. Make sure you know where you're going and that you've sussed out the safest route to a shelter or a friend's house.

Don't go for a paddle. Never try to walk through floodwater. A paltry 15 cm of water is enough to knock you off your feet. Besides, the water may be deeper than it looks and the ground underneath may have been washed away.

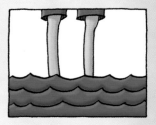

Don't go for a swim. Swimming in fast-flowing floodwater is a desperately dodgy thing to do. Chances are you'll be swept away or hit by debris floating in the water.

Don't camp on a riverbank. Even if it's dry now, a flash flood can start flowing in minutes and wash you away. Get to high ground immediately ... but watch out for mudslides set off by swollen streams.

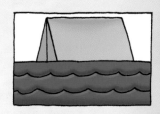

AFTER...

Wait for the all clear. This means the water's going down and flood watches and warnings are no longer in force. But double check it's safe to go home.

Start mopping up. Clean and dry out your home as quickly as possible. Mould is a serious menace after a flood. Take up wet carpets and clean everything thoroughly with disinfectant.

Don't drink the water. It might be contaminated with sewage and chock-full of germs that can make you seriously ill. Boil any water you use until you know it's safe to turn on the tap. Throw away any food that's been in contact with floodwater.

Watch out for snakes. Floods may flush snakes and other animals out of their homes and into yours. Use a stick to poke through debris when you go back indoors.

SURVIVAL TIP

Never go for a drive through floodwater, whatever you do. Your car can quickly become a death trap. More than half of all the people who die in floods are killed when their cars get swept away. And woe betide you if you break down. By the time the water reaches the windows, the water pressure will be so great that you won't be able to open the doors...

Could you stop a flood in mid-flow?

Floods aren't just fatal. They're horribly fickle, too. Even if you know when a flood's likely to happen, you can't really stop it in full flow. But that doesn't stop hydrologists trying out ways of keeping floods at bay. Which of these flood-proof measures do you think would work best?

A) A wall.
B) A dam.
C) A tree..

DAM!

Answers:
In fact, they'd all do the trick, though some have been more successful than others at stopping the flood and reducing the damage it does.

a) A wall or embankment on each bank of the river is sometimes called a levee. Levee is the French word for 'raised'. Levees make the bank higher and stop water from overflowing on to the floodplain. But what happens if a levee springs a leak? This is what happened in 1993 when the Mississippi River burst its banks with catastrophic results (see page 67).

RIVER   FLOOD LEVEL   LEVEE

b) Dams are handy for stopping rivers from flooding. The water collects behind the dam in a reservoir and is released slowly to prevent a surge downstream. What's more, all that water can be used for drinking, farming and generating cheap electricity. Trouble is, they're not always watertight. In 1976, the Teton Dam on Snake River, Idaho, USA, collapsed, flooding 65 square km and leaving 30,000 people homeless.

c) Plants trap rain through their leaves, and their roots help bind the soil together. But, in some places, flooding is made worse because plants and trees have been cut down. So there's nothing to stop rain racing into the river. The rain also washes loose soil into the river, making the riverbed deeper and the river more likely to overflow.

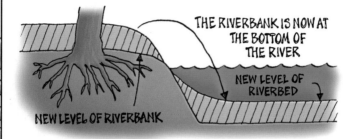

THE RIVERBANK IS NOW AT THE BOTTOM OF THE RIVER

NEW LEVEL OF RIVERBED

NEW LEVEL OF RIVERBANK

BLOWING
HOT AND COLD

If you find yourself wilting in summer and shivering in winter, you might want to give this chapter a miss. It's all about wicked weather that blows horribly hot and catastrophically cold. Get stuck in a heatwave and you won't just feel hot and bothered. You'll be struck down by deadly heatstroke. And beware if a blizzard bites. Forget snowball fights with your friends. After all, you won't be able to make a snowball if frostbite's made your fingers drop off.
Still feeling hardy enough to brave the weather at its worst? To help you get back in one piece, here are some red-hot (and stone-cold) survival tips.

WICKED WEATHER REPORT

A heatwave is a long stretch of scorching-hot weather, often with high humidity. So it not only feels horribly hot but also horribly sticky. In North America, a heatwave's usually said to be three days in a row with temperatures above 32.2°C. But it can get a whole lot hotter than that. When a heatwave hit the USA in 2006, temperatures reached a baking 48°C.

HEATWAVE FACTS:

• Heatwaves can be lethal. In the USA alone, over 2,000 people died from the heat between 1992 and 2001. That's 14 times more than were killed in hurricanes.

• It's not just the heat that's a killer. When the wind drops, dirt and fumes hang around in the air, making it hard to breathe.

• Heatwaves have some other serious side effects, such as ruined crops and catastrophic wildfires.

Horrible heatwaves...

Britain, 1976

In 1976, Britain was blasted by the hottest summer on record. Temperatures reached 27°C everyday, and soared to 36°C on 3 July. To make matters worse, the country was suffering from a dreadful drought. In some places, water ran short and devastating forest fires broke out. One fire burned 50,000 trees to the ground.

Fortunately, in the last week of August, massive thunderstorms brought rain for the first time in weeks.

Australia, 1994

Over the last 100 years, heatwaves have killed over 4,000 people in Australia – more than any other natural hazard. In 1994, Australia was hit by the hottest December day for 40 years. Temperatures reached a sizzling 44°C and many people were treated for heat exhaustion and dehydration. Other problems were caused by deadly air pollution, and road surfaces and overhead wires melting in the heat.

USA, 1995

One of the deadliest heatwaves ever hit Chicago in July and August. Almost 600 people were killed in just five days when temperatures soared to a scorching 41°C. Things were made worse because Chicago is a big city and its buildings simply soaked up heat, so it got hotter and hotter. But people also blamed city officials for the tragically high death toll. They didn't issue a heat warning until the last day of the heat wave.

IT'S OFFICIAL...THIS WEATHER IS NOW CLASSED AS A HEATWAVE...

WICKED WEATHER REPORT

A blizzard is a wicked winter storm, but not just any old winter storm. To count as a blizzard, it needs three things: temperatures below −12°C, heavy snow and icy winds. The winds roar at over 70 km/h, blasting the snow along. Never mind the nose in front of your face. In these teeth-chattering conditions, you won't be able to see a thing.

BLIZZARD FACTS:
- Blizzards can cause dreadful damage, burying cars, trucks and even trains under tonnes of snow, and bringing cities to a standstill.
- The worst place for blizzards is Antarctica, where the wind howls off the ice at speeds of at least 160 km/h.
- If freezing-cold temperatures weren't enough, the wind makes it feel even colder. And the stronger the wind, the colder it feels.

Blizzard blasts New York

Eastern USA, March 1888

On 11 March, the weather in New York City was warm and wet for the time of year. But it didn't last long. Next day, the heavy rain turned to snow, temperatures plummeted and a biting wind whipped up. Soon a full-scale blizzard was raging, plunging the unprepared city into chaos. 'The Great White Hurricane', as it was known, blasted the whole of the east coast and more than 400 people lost their lives. Ships were sunk, telephone wires cut and transport ground to a halt. New York was hit hardest of all.

A metre of snow fell over the city, piling up into drifts over 10 metres high. The East River froze over and people were able to walk across it from Brooklyn to Manhattan. Some people who went out in the blizzard had strange tales to tell. One man cut his forehead on a horse's hoof when he fell into a drift. He didn't know a dead horse was buried in the snow. Another man was struggling home and leant against a lamppost for a rest. Before he knew it, he'd fallen asleep and his face had frozen against the post. When he finally woke up and staggered home, he realized his false teeth were missing. He later found them stuck to the ice on the lamppost.

The blizzard lasted for three long days before, at last, the snow began to thaw. By that time, 100 people in New York had died and many more were starving as the stores ran out of food. It was the worst storm the city had ever known.

First-Aid Manual: Hot and Cold Weather

Heat Exhaustion

Symptoms: You sweat buckets but your skin feels cool. You feel sick, dizzy and worn out. You also have a splitting headache. But your body temperature is normal (37°C). It's not as serious as heatstroke but you'll still feel horribly ill.

Treatment: Get out of the heat and into a cooler place. Loosen or take off tight clothes. Wrap yourself in a wet sheet or towel. Slowly sip a glass of cool water every 15 minutes but stop if you feel sick.

Heatstroke

Symptoms: Hot, red, dry skin and high pulse rate. Shallow breathing. Very high body temperature (39-40°C). You'll feel as if you're burning up. Eventually, you'll collapse and lose consciousness. Unless you get help fast, you'll die.

Treatment: Get to a cooler place and sit in a cool bath. Or you can wrap yourself in wet sheets or splash yourself cool water if there isn't a bathroom handy. Wrap icepacks in a cloth and put them on your wrists and ankles. Lie down, near a fan if you can, and try to keep cool until help arrives.

Hypothermia

Symptoms: Uncontrollable shivering, slowly at first, then faster and faster. You'll feel drowsy and get confused. You'll start to slur your words and you'll stumble if you try to walk. If you don't warm up quickly, you'll curl up into a ball and possibly die.

Treatment: You need to wrap up warm in extra clothes or a blanket, covering up your head and neck. And you need to get moving to get your circulation flowing. However sluggish you feel. You can sit down now and then for a nice bowl of hot soup.

Frostbite

Symptoms: It's when your skin and flesh get so cold that they freeze solid. Your fingers, toes, earlobes and nose are most at risk. First they'll start tingling, and then they'll go cold and white. Then they'll go numb. Eventually, they may go hard and black, and drop off.

Treatment: You need to thaw out the frostbitten bits but don't rub them. Dunk them in warm (not hot) water for an hour or so. When the skin turns red and swollen, you'll know it's warmed up enough. But be warned – this bit will be horribly painful.

HOW TO SURVIVE A HEATWAVE...

DRINK PLENTY OF WATER:
EVEN IF YOU'RE NOT FEELING THIRSTY.
IT'LL STOP YOU GETTING DEHYDRATED
(SEE SURVIVAL TIP)

STAY INDOORS:
AS MUCH AS POSSIBLE. IF YOU'VE GOT IT,
TURN ON THE AIR-CONDITIONING. IF NOT,
GO TO THE LOWEST ROOM YOU CAN, LIKE A
BASEMENT. HEAT RISES SO YOU'LL BE
COOLER THERE. TAKE A SHOWER, OR SOAK
YOUR FEET IN A BUCKET OF COLD WATER

STAY INSIDE:
KEEP PLENTY OF WARM CLOTHES AND BLANKETS HANDY. SHUT OFF ANY ROOMS YOU DON'T USE AND STUFF TOWELS OR NEWSPAPERS IN CRACKS UNDER THE DOORS TO STOP DRAUGHTS. CHECK THE WEATHER FORECAST BEFORE YOU GO OUT

DIG A SNOW CAVE:
TO PROTECT YOU FROM THE WIND. DON'T EAT THE SNOW, EVEN IF YOU'RE THIRSTY. IT'LL LOWER YOUR TEMPERATURE AND MAKE YOU FEEL COLDER

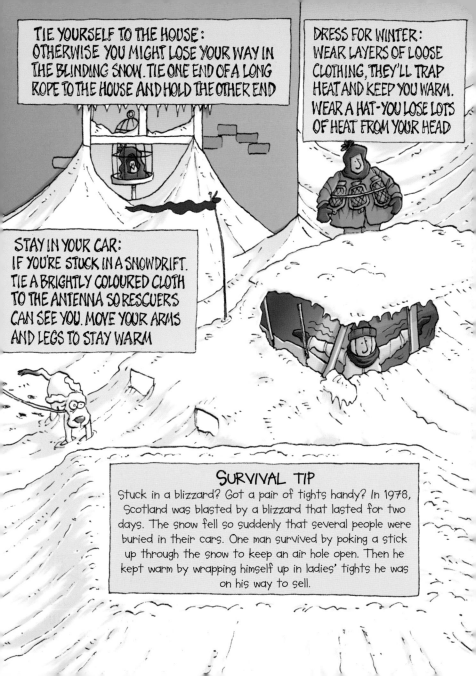

EPILOGUE

Congratulations! You've braved the most wicked weather on the planet on your whirlwind tour. You've done the twist with a tornado and hung on for dear life as a hurricane shot through, and you're not even wet or windswept. Well, not very much. But before you decide to raise the roof and set off on a tornado-chasing tour, here's a frightening thought. If you thought the weather in this book was wicked enough, think again. In the future, it's likely to get much wilder. And it's all down to something called global warming…

WICKED WEATHER REPORT

Name of weather: GLOBAL WARMING
What it is: THE WAY THE EARTH'S CLIMATE IS GETTING WARMER

HOW IT HAPPENS:

1 Tonnes of gases like carbon dioxide are pumped into the atmosphere. It comes from cars and lorries, factories and burning rainforest trees. It's also the stuff you breathe out.

2 These gases are called greenhouse gases because they trap heat coming from the Sun. Like the glass in a greenhouse.

3 Trouble is, the amount of gases is growing. And they're trapping too much heat, making the Earth worryingly warm.

GLOBAL WARMING FACTS:

● Without greenhouse gases, the Earth would be covered in ice and too parky to live on.

● By the year 2050, the amount of carbon dioxide in the atmosphere might have doubled.

● Scientists reckon that by 2050 the Earth may have heated up by about 2°C. Sounds pretty paltry but it could be enough to drive the weather wild.

● Humans aren't only to blame for global warming. Tonnes of pongy methane (another ghastly gas) are given off in cows' farts and burps.

Wilder weather

So if the Earth's in the grip of global warming, what might it mean for the weather? Here are some possible knock-on effects:

More hurricanes?

If the oceans warm up, it might mean more places where hurricanes can form. Some scientists reckon hurricanes are getting stronger, with more Category 5 storms possible. They'll also be likely to last longer and get trickier to forecast.

More floods?

Global warming might mean parts of the world get wetter with heavier downpours of rain. And the bad news doesn't stop there. Freak downpours might lead to more floods and more mudslides – with disastrous effects.

More tornadoes?

Wild weather might whip up more thunderstorms ... and more tornadoes. In fact, scientists reckon the rot's already set in. In 2004, a staggering 1,722 tornadoes hit the USA. That's a whole 500 more than in a normal year.

More heatwaves?

In 2006, a fantastically fierce heatwave left Europe and the USA reeling. And it looks like it won't be the last. Heatwaves may happen more often, last twice as long, and what's worse, feel even more sweltering.

So, the weather's all set to get wilder. At least, that's what some of the experts think. And they blame global warming for the doom and gloom. But not everyone agrees. There's even one theory that global warming is making it harder for hurricanes to form. Other scientists reckon the changes in the weather are all down to natural events (rather than horrible humans). They say storms go in cycles, so every few years it gets wilder, and then it calms down again. One thing's for certain – something strange seems to be happening to the weather and worse may yet be to come. So it's best to be prepared. Just in case wicked weather's on the way, make sure you've stocked up on emergency supplies and know where you've put the storm-cellar key. Looks like you're going to need them.

INDEX

Enjoyed

WICKED WEATHER?

Want to get your teeth
into more Horrible
Geography Handbooks?

WILD ANIMALS

is in the shops
NOW!